ZOOM IN!

For over 50 years, Guinness World Records has documented the world's most amazing record-breakers in every field imaginable. Today, the records in their archives number more than 40,000.

In this collection, we'll zoom in on 25 record-holders in the animal kingdoms of sea, land, and sky. Beneath the waves, we'll spy on the most poisonous mollusk. Crawling ashore, we'll climb inside the largest nest built by a land mammal. We'll snack with the most destructive insect before taking wing alongside the rarest bird of prey. Finally, we'll visit five superstar record-holders that are the "Best of the Best!"

Go up close and get wild — Guinness World Records style!

A Record-Breaking History

The idea for Guinness World Records grew out of a question. In 1951, Sir Hugh Beaver, the managing director of the Guinness Brewery, wanted to know which was the fastest game bird in Europe — the golden plover or the grouse? Some people argued that it was the grouse. Others claimed it was the plover. A book to settle the debate did not exist until Sir Hugh discovered the knowledgeable twin brothers Norris and Ross McWhirter, who lived in London.

Like their father and grandfather, the McWhirter twins loved information. They were kids just like you when they started clipping interesting facts from newspapers and memorizing important dates in world history. As well as learning the names of every river, mountain range, and nation's capital, they knew the record for pole squatting (196 days in 1954), which language had only one irregular verb (Turkish), and that the grouse — flying at a timed speed of 43.5 miles per hour — is faster than the golden plover at 40.4 miles per hour.

Norris and Ross served in the Royal Navy during World War II, graduated from college, and launched their own fact-finding business called McWhirter Twins, Ltd. They were the perfect people to compile the book of records that Sir Hugh Beaver searched for yet could not find.

The first edition of *The Guinness Book of Records* was published on August 27, 1955, and since then has been published in 37 languages and more than 100 countries. In 2000, the book title changed to *Guinness World Records* and has set an incredible record of its own: Excluding non-copyrighted books such as the Bible and the Koran, *Guinness World Records* is the best-selling book of all time!

Today, the official Keeper of the Records keeps a careful eye on each Guinness World Record, compiling and verifying the greatest the world has to offer — from the fastest and the tallest to the slowest and the smallest, with everything in between.

GUINNESS WORLD RECORDS

UP CLOSE

Astonishing Animals

Compiled by Joanne Mattern and Ryan Herndon

For Guinness World Records: Laura Barrett, Craig Glenday,
Kim Lacey, Stuart Claxton, Betty Halvagi

SCHOLASTIC INC.
New York Toronto London Auckland Sydney
Mexico City New Delhi Hong Kong Buenos Aires

Guinness World Records Limited has a very thorough accreditation system for records verification. However, while every effort is made to ensure accuracy, Guinness World Records Limited cannot be held responsible for any errors contained in this work. Feedback from our readers on any point of accuracy is always welcomed.

© 2005 Guinness World Records Limited, a HIT Entertainment Limited Company.

Published by Scholastic Inc. SCHOLASTIC and associated logos are trademarks and/or registered trademarks of Scholastic Inc.

ISBN 0-439-71568-7

Designed by Michelle Martinez Design, Inc.
Photo Research by Els Rijper
Records from the Archives of Guinness World Records

12 11 10 9 8 7 6 5 4 3 2 1   5 6 7 8 9 10/0

Printed in the U.S.A.

First printing, December 2005

Visit Guinness World Records at www.guinnessworldrecords.com

Salty Sea Life

The underwater world is a mysterious and fascinating place. It is also home to billions of creatures. Weird and astonishing wildlife swim, hunt, and breathe beneath the waves. Put on your flippers — we're about to go diving deep into the big blue sea!

Stars sparkle overhead . . . and beneath the waves.

A fascinating sea creature is the starfish (or sea star). Not truly a fish because it lacks vertebrae and fins, starfish belong to a group named echinoderms, which means "spiny skin" in Greek.

Humans cannot sprout a replacement for an injured limb. Yet if a fish nibbles off a starfish's arm, the starfish can grow a brand-new one exactly like its other four, six, or twenty arms! Some sea stars can grow a whole new starfish from just one severed ray.

Starfish come in many sizes and colors. The record-holders are even smaller and bigger than these specimens!

RECORD 1
Largest and Smallest Starfish

The **Largest Starfish**, out of 1,600 known contenders, is the brisingid (*Midgardia xandaros*), measuring from tip to tip at an impressive 4 feet 6 inches. Super-sized doesn't mean super-sturdy. Examiners aboard the Texas A&M University research vessel *The Alaminos* took extra care collecting this extremely fragile specimen from the Gulf of Mexico in 1968.

At the scale's opposite end is the asterinid sea star (*Patiriella parvivipara*). The **Smallest Starfish** was discovered in 1975, on the west coast of Eyre Peninsula, South Australia. Its radius was only 0.18 inches, and its diameter was less than 0.35 inches.

A starfish's arm is a ray. Its tube feet are podia.

WATER POWER

Although it is symmetrical (both sides of its body are the same), a starfish does not have a front or back. Unlike humans, starfish move off in any direction without turning around. An internal hydraulic system propels the starfish across the ocean floor. It sucks water into its body through a valve located on its top side. The water is then pumped through valves on its underside. This system helps the starfish cling on to a rock so tightly that it's almost impossible to pry off — a good survival trait if a hungry predator is doing the tugging.

FACT:

If you're a clam, avoid starfish! Some starfish species can engulf a clam's shell and pry it open with their water-powered arms. Then the starfish slides its stomach inside the clam's shell for a hearty meal. Talk about take-out food!

UP CLOSE

Favorite appetizers of animals and humans form the mollusks group.

Oysters, scallops, and mussels are shell cousins of the clam and are called bivalves, which means they have two shells. A large interior muscle opens and closes the shell.

Pearls form when a piece of sand or other particle irritates the inside of the shell. The clam secretes a hard substance called *nacre*. In time, the layers of nacre cover the irritant and create a pearl. An oyster's pearl is more valuable than one from a clam.

Pearls form if sand or other irritants get trapped inside.

RECORD 2
Largest Clam

You might have seen old horror movies where deep-sea divers are gobbled up by giant clams. Although this is strictly science fiction, there are indeed monstrous-sized clams dwelling on the reefs of the Western Pacific and Indian Oceans. The **Largest Clam** is the appropriately named marine giant clam. This mollusk usually grows to be more than 3 feet wide and can weigh up to 660 pounds. It eats plankton and algae. The record-holder measured 4 feet long and weighed 734 pounds!

The sea horse's Greek name, *Hippocampus,* means "bent horse."

RECORD 3
Slowest Fish

Horses will not win every race, especially underwater. The **Slowest Fish** is the sea horse. Its top speed is 0.001 miles per hour. Why so slow? A sea horse has a rigid body structure. Its pectoral and dorsal fins propel it along, but it swims in one position: upright. A weak current will sweep away these poor swimmers, unless the sea horse lassos the nearest coral and marine plants using its curly tail.

Approximately 35 species of sea horse swim in the temperate and tropical waters of the Caribbean, the Mediterranean Sea, and parts of the Atlantic, Pacific, and Indian Oceans.

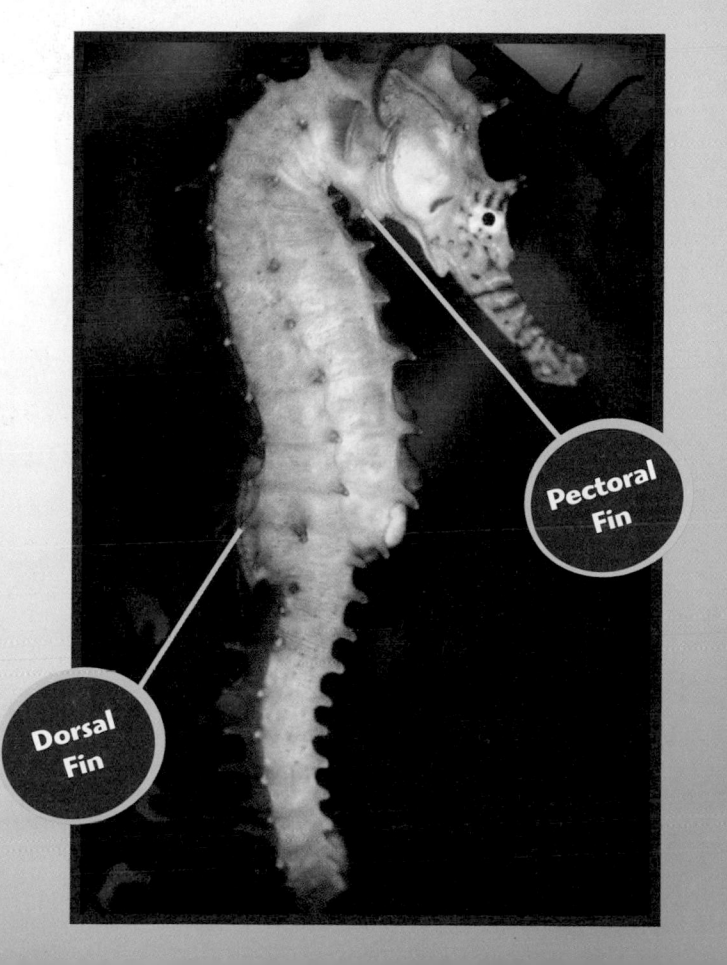

Pectoral Fin

Dorsal Fin

UNDERCOVER

A sea horse's body may not be great for swimming, but it's perfect for hiding! Small-sized at 2 to 14 inches long in beautiful camouflage colors, the sea horse is an expert at disguise. It can stand up straight among coral branches, anchored by its tail. Its shape and color help it appear to be part of the coral. While it hides from other fish that might eat it, the sea horse sucks up its own meals of tiny plankton and fish larvae.

Where Sea Horses Swim

Here's one animal that can hurt you if you get too close!

These octopuses don't seek out humans. Usually their toxin knocks out their favorite meal: crabs. Its distinctive blue rings mark the octopus as a water hazard. Other sea creatures, and humans, should heed nature's warning signs and steer clear!

RECORD 4
Most Venomous Mollusk

A bite from the **Most Venomous Mollusk** hardly hurts . . . until the poison in its saliva kills you within minutes! The venom of the blue-ringed octopus is neurotoxic, a poison that attacks and paralyzes its victim's nervous system, including the ability to breathe. Two closely related species have been found around the coasts of Australia and in parts of Southeast Asia. These small creatures — about 4 inches long — carry enough venom each to paralyze 10 adult humans.

UP CLOSE

LIFE IN THE CROWD

These little animals are the basic diet for whales, seals, fish, squid, and seabirds. In turn, they eat creatures even smaller! Copepods feed on plankton, tiny animals and plants that drift through the water. Copepods grab plankton with their legs and push them into their mouths. One species of copepod can eat almost 375,000 plankton in a 24-hour period!

RECORD 5
Most Abundant Animal

Here's a sea creature that won't get lost in a crowd. It IS a crowd! The one-eyed copepod is a tiny crustacean that is the **Most Abundant Animal**. More than a trillion individuals can form just one group! There are about 12,000 species of copepods. They can be found almost everywhere where there's water. Copepods are super small — they range between just 0.04 to 0.4 inches long.

FACT:

A copepod's body has three parts. Its abdomen has five segments. Its thorax has six segments. The third part is its head. The whole body is shaped like a cylinder and is narrower in the back than in the front. There is a pair of long antennae at the top of the head. These antennae are used to float in place without exerting a lot of energy. The copepod uses its several pairs of swimming legs to move through the water.

Wading ashore, let's explore the land we walk upon. The largest land mammal offers plenty of seating space upon its shoulders. We'll hunt with striped and furry man-eaters. As night falls, we'll settle down inside a nest roomy enough for two, before rising bright-eyed and bushy-tailed to build new habitats with the engineers of the animal kingdom.

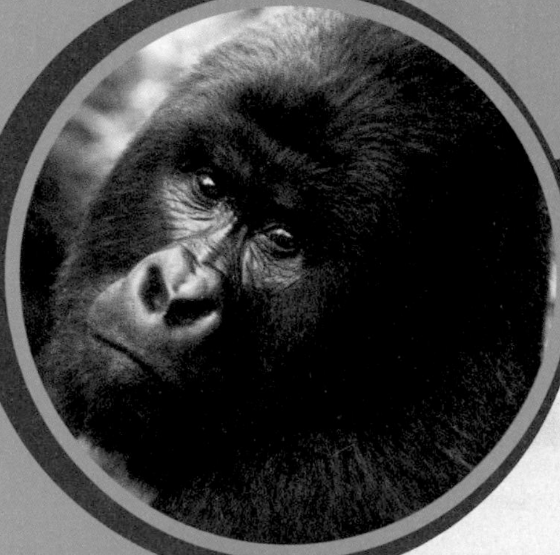

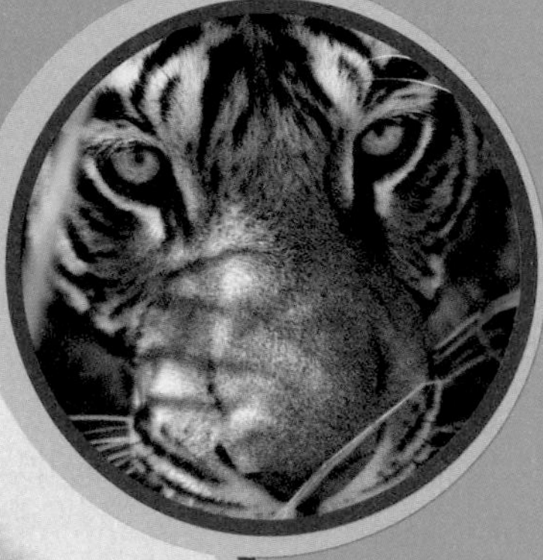

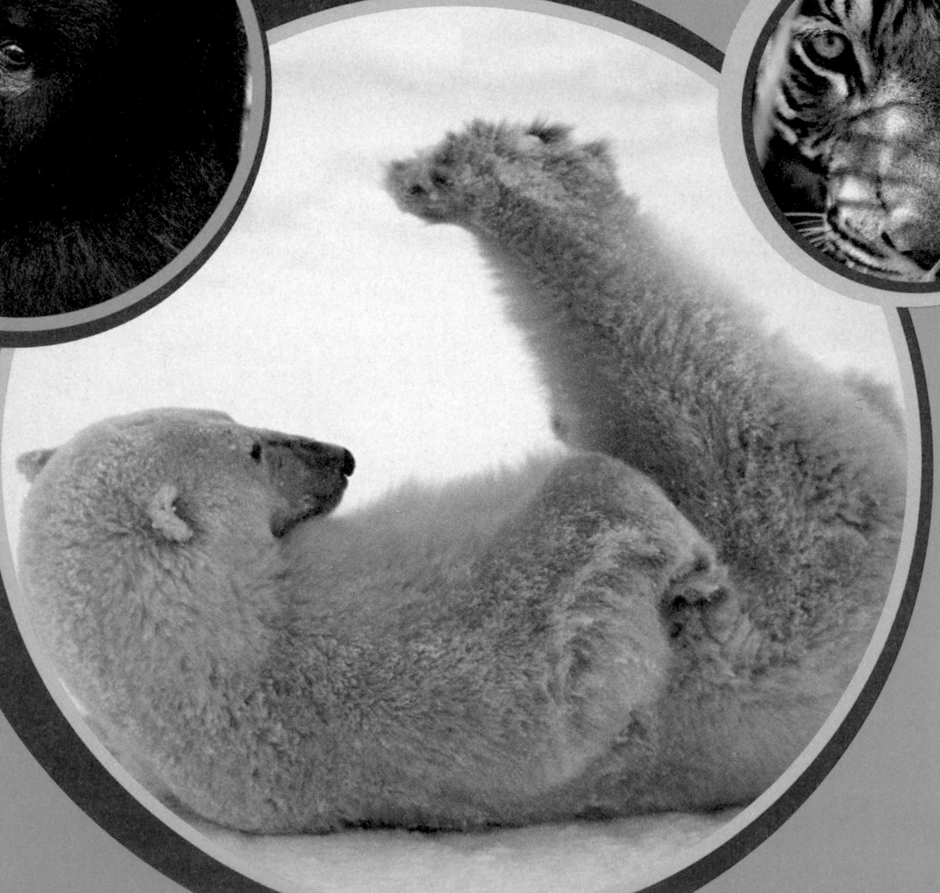

RECORD 6
Largest Land Mammal

It takes a big animal to carry a big record. The **Largest Land Mammal** is the adult male African bush elephant. On average, this species stands 9 feet 10 inches to 12 feet 2 inches at the shoulder and weighs 8,800 to 15,400 pounds. The record-holder measured 13 feet 7 inches in a line from the highest point of the shoulder to the base of the forefoot, which works out to a standing height of about 12 feet 11 inches. These pachyderms are vegetarians and can eat up to 300 pounds of food a day. An elephant's skin alone weighs almost a ton!

TOOTHY

Asian, or Indian, elephants are a little smaller in body — and ear size — than their African cousins. Only male Asian elephants have large overgrown teeth, unlike both male and female African elephants.

The Longest Tusks are from an African elephant preserved at the Bronx Zoo in New York City. The right tusk measures 11 feet 5.5 inches along the outside curve, while the left tusk measures 11 feet. The combined weight of both tusks is a whopping 293 pounds!

The Heaviest Tusks of a male African elephant from Kenya weighed 240 pounds and 225 pounds!

Camouflage is important when you're sneaking up on someone.

The idea is to blend in with the colors of your environment. A tiger's body is designed for hunting. Its stripes make this meat-eater nearly invisible in the long grass and among the shadows when stalking its prey. Its back legs are longer than its front legs, able to push the cat farther during its powerful spring and pounce. Its shoulders are heavily muscled, critical in pulling its fleeing prey down to the ground. Its large paws have long, sharp claws, all the better to snare its meal with. The tiger's strong jaw finishes the job with a fierce bite.

RECORD 7
Largest Feline Carnivore

"Big cats" are large-sized wild felines, such as lions, cheetahs, leopards, and tigers. The term distinguishes them from the normal-sized kitty cats people keep as family pets in their homes. The Siberian tiger is the **Largest Feline Carnivore**. These big cats can measure up to 11 feet long and weigh up to 800 pounds. Their natural habitats are the forests of eastern Asia, northern China, and Manchuria.

FACT:

Tiger cubs are born blind, helpless, and weigh 2 pounds. After 18 months, the young tigers are on their own.

HOMEMAKERS

There are few tigers left in the wild. That's because people inhabit areas that were once a tiger's domain, by building homes and roads. However, humans are also saving tiger species from extinction, by building sanctioned areas for these magnificent cats. Tigers breed easily in captivity and you can visit zoos to safely see these carnivores dining, up close!

The **Largest Tiger Litter Born in Captivity** was 6 Bengal white tiger cubs on November 18, 2003, in the Buenos Aires Zoo, Argentina.

Hunters come in many species, from stalking tigers to shaggy bears in the snow. Polar bears are just as serious about hunting as tigers, and they start training their young at an early age. During the fall, pregnant polar bears dig a den in the snow. They stay in the den through the winter and give birth to 1 to 3 cubs. In the spring, the family emerges and the lessons begin. The female nurses her cubs for about 2 years and 6 months while teaching them how to hunt. When old enough, the polar bears lumber off to continue the mighty hunting tradition.

RECORD 8
Largest Land Carnivore

This bear is the extra-large meat-eater variety. The adult male polar bear is the **Largest Land Carnivore**. Its digestive system is able to process meat better than plants, making the polar bear the most carnivorous of the bear species. This fierce hunter measures 7 feet 11 inches to 8 feet 6 inches from nose to tail. It weighs 880 to 1,320 pounds before any of its super-sized meals. The polar bear has successfully hunted walruses (1,100 pounds) and the world's **Largest Prey**, beluga whales (1,320 pounds).

The stomach capacity of a polar bear is 150 pounds.

SEAL THE MEAL

Polar bears live in the frozen north of our planet, in an area called the Arctic. Seals are a favorite meal. Hunting methods include:

- Stake out the seal's breathing hole in the ice. When the seal surfaces for air . . . pounce!

- Stroll across the sea ice . . . or slide and catch a fleeing meal. Polar bears have been spotted hundreds of miles from shore.

- Swim for your breakfast, lunch, and dinner. Polar bears will swim 60 miles to hunt seals.

Polar bears can smell a seal 20 miles away!

People and primates are closely related.

We live in communities, raise our young, take care of our old, build and relocate homes, and communicate in a language understood by our species. Let's investigate the primates' constant construction and relocation of their roomy, cozy homes.

Largest Mammal to Build a Nest

Birds are not the only animals that build nests. The **Largest Mammal to Build a Nest** is the gorilla (*Gorilla gorilla*) of Africa. Adult male gorillas can grow up to 5 feet 9 inches tall and weigh 300–500 pounds. Big animals need big beds! Gorillas build a new nest every day using leaves and branches. This circular nest measures on average 3 feet 3 inches in diameter. Unlike the birds' nests, these nests stay on the ground.

UP CLOSE

FACT:

Gorillas are vegetarians and eat plants, berries, and leaves.

Koko has a pet kitten.

SIGNS FOR KOKO

During the 1970s, researchers began using American Sign Language to communicate with gorillas. Their best pupil was Koko, the Gorilla Most Proficient in Sign Language.

Koko was born at the San Francisco Zoo. Her teacher, Dr. Francine Patterson, started sign language instruction with Koko in 1972. By 2000, Koko had a vocabulary of more than 1,000 signs and could understand about 2,000 words of spoken English. Koko's command of the language is so good that she can argue, joke, make up her own signs, and tell a few fibs.

Gnaw a log with the sharp-toothed engineers of the animal kingdom.

Follow the tracks to see how beavers build brand-new habitats and forests.

- Beaver dams, constructed from cut trees, create ponds and marshy areas.

- Different trees take root.

- Wildlife moves into this altered area's habitat.

- Time passes, and a beaver pond becomes a meadow.

- Growing shrubs provide shade for more tree seedlings to sprout.

- Shrubs die out beneath the shade cast by growing trees.

- A forest is born.

The lodge's underwater entrance foils predators.

RECORD 10
Largest Structure Built by a Land Animal

Beavers build log-homes in Canadian and American rivers and streams. Their "chain saws" are long, sharp teeth. They gnaw around the tree trunk until — TIMBER! — the tree falls. Beavers carry or float the logs down the river, stack them up, then add mud, wood, vegetation, and stones to create the **Largest Structure Built by a Land Animal**. Beaver dams can be up to 5 feet wide. The longest covered 0.9 miles. The beavers quickly patch any leaks. The dam blocks off the river's flow and a private pond forms. The beavers use sticks and mud to construct a lodge in the middle of the pond, where they live during the winter. The largest lodge ever recorded was 40 feet across and 16 feet high.

People have strong reactions to reptiles and insects. Some scream in delight, others in fright. Take a closer look at the ground. What would the world look like to you if you were crawling around on your belly, or flitting from tree leaf to cornstalk? Slither among the heavy and lengthy constrictors, then dash off with the speedy iguana. It's time to get wild and wiggly.

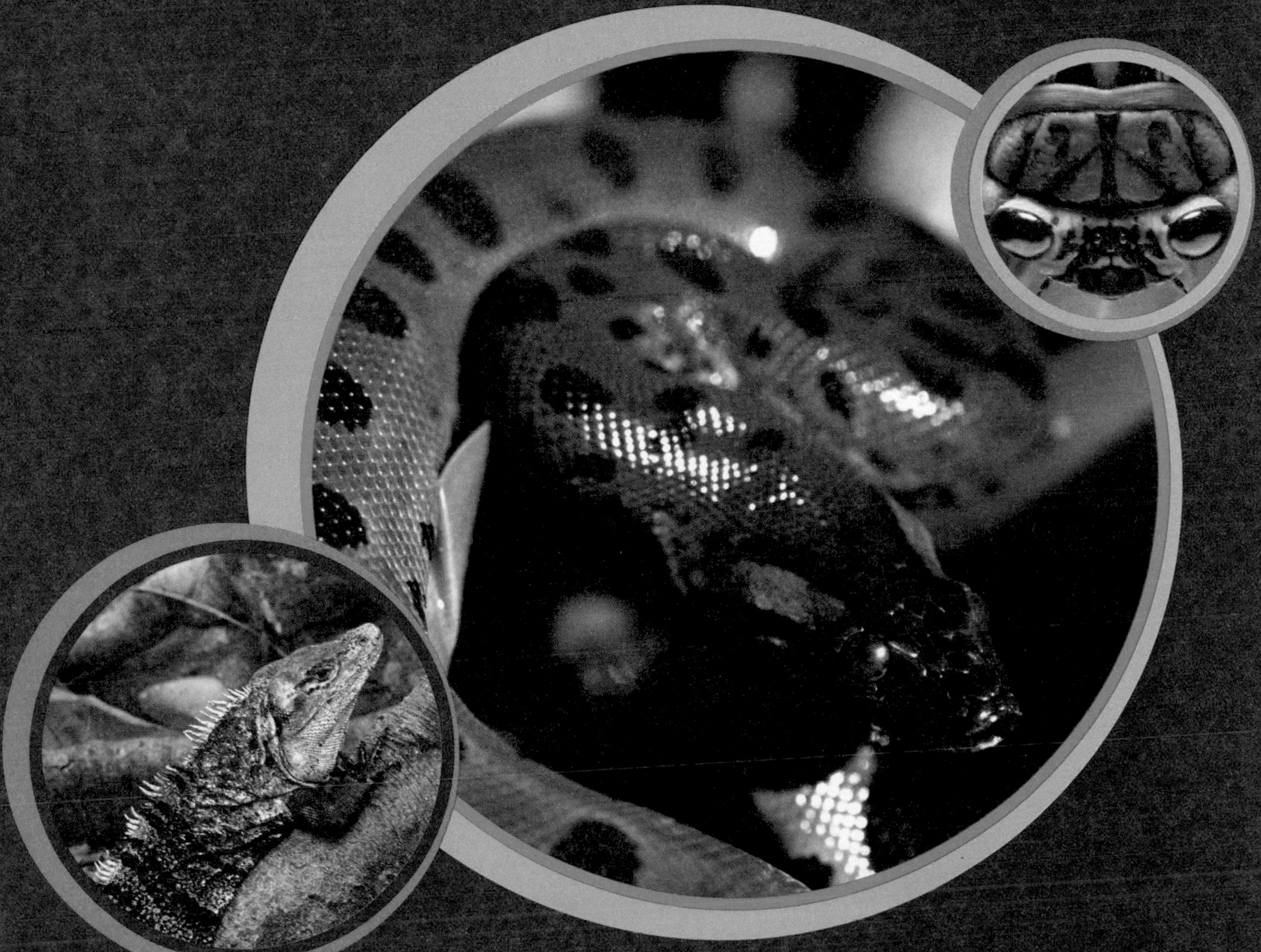

Confused about which snake is wrapped around you?

Anacondas are a species of boa constrictor while pythons are a separate snake group called *Pythonidae*. Pythons are found mostly in Africa, Asia, and Australia. Offspring hatch from eggs. Anacondas live in the same areas plus North, Central, and South America. Offspring are born straight from the snake. These gigantic snakes are nonvenomous, but they suffocate you within their coils before swallowing you in one long GULP!

RECORD 11
Heaviest Snake

The **Heaviest Snake** is the green anaconda of South America and Trinidad. It is normally 18-20 feet long. A female anaconda found in Brazil in 1960 measured a tremendous 27 feet 7 inches long. She was 44 inches around — equal to an adult man's waist size — and weighed an estimated 500 pounds.

The **Heaviest Living Snake** is a Burmese python named Baby who lives in the Serpent Safari Park in Gurnee, Illinois. Baby measured 27 feet long, 28 inches around, and weighed 403 pounds on November 20, 1998. Pythons continue to grow, so Baby is even bigger now!

The **Longest Snake** was a reticulated python measuring 32 feet 9.5 inches, found in 1912 in Celebes, Indonesia.

RATTLE ME THIS

The **Heaviest Venomous Snake** is America's own eastern diamondback rattlesnake, slithering in the southeastern United States. It weighs 12 to 15 pounds and measures 5 to 6 feet long. The largest specimen found weighed 34 pounds and was 7 feet 9 inches long. The rattle, a snake's warning alarm to others, is made of interlocking rings of keratin — the same material as our fingernails.

FACT:

Rattlesnakes try to avoid large predators, such as humans, more often than looking for a fight. If bitten, always seek medical attention immediately.

UP CLOSE

FACT:

Rattlesnakes are important members of the ecosystem because they control rodent populations.

Mothers can be the fiercest protectors, whether human or reptile.

A female iguana digs her nest hole in the ground, deposits between 2 and 25 eggs, and defends her home from other females. The babies hatch 3 to 4 months later, and must dig their own way out of the hole. After about a week, the lizards emerge. If they can survive the first few years, these lizards can live up to 60 years.

RECORD 12
Fastest Lizard

If a bunch of lizards held a race, the spiny-tailed iguana (*Ctenosaura*) from Central America would be the **Fastest Lizard**. These reptiles run standing up on their back legs and clock in at 21.7 miles per hour. That's about 4 times faster than a human can walk! Adult males can grow to 18 inches long, with an *additional* 18 inches of tail. These lizards eat a lot of fruit, but they also chase down and eat mice, bats, frogs, small birds, and insects. These iguanas will even eat their own eggs, and the tail of a young iguana was once found in the stomach of an adult male. No wonder the iguana starts running at an early age!

Sharp, curved spines ring the tail of the spiny-tailed iguana.

STICK BUG

Insects outnumber humans, yet some species of bugs are in danger of being wiped out forever. A stick insect can hide in plain sight — it looks exactly like a stick — and camouflages itself in a bush or on a tree. This ability has helped its species survive for millions of years, even before the dinosaurs walked the earth or scientists looked closer at that odd stick with eyes.

RECORD 13
Rarest Insect

Scientists had concluded that the Lord Howe Island stick insect had been extinct for 80 years. Black rats colonizing the island in 1918 were blamed for the insect's disappearance. Instead, the smart bug was in hiding. In February 2001, a tiny colony and several eggs were discovered under a bush. In 2003, a rescue team captured 2 breeding pairs and brought them to the Melbourne Zoo in Australia. The pair laid more than 100 eggs, and the first hatched in September 2003.

Today, scientists believe 10 specimens of the **Rarest Insect** live on the remote island off the coast of Australia.

Stick insects can grow to be up to 6 inches long, and 0.5 inches thick.

Sound affects different species in various ways.

A sound that humans label noise can be the most romantic song . . . for a bug.

The life span of most cicadas is 30 to 40 days. The species must mate and lay eggs before dying. A male cicada vibrates a special part of its body called tymbal organs to attract a female. These organs vibrate more than 7,400 times a minute, producing that one-of-a-kind cicada buzz.

RECORD 14
Loudest Insect

Could you please keep it down out there? That's what you might ask an African cicada, but the **Loudest Insect** has a time limit on its song. The cicada's calling song measures 106.7 decibels at a distance of 19.5 inches. If you stand right next to the cicada, the measurement is closer to 110 decibels. That's as loud as sitting in the front row of a rock concert! You can hear their ear-ringing racket from a quarter of a mile away.

RECORD 15

Most Destructive Insect

Don't be fooled by an insect's miniscule size. Bugs can do BIG damage! The **Most Destructive Insect** is only 1.8 to 2.4 inches long, but its appetite destroys lives. Desert locusts can eat their own weight in food every day. They live in Africa, the Middle East, and Asia, and travel in enormous groups called swarms. A "small" swarm of 50 million locusts can eat enough food to sustain 500 people for an entire year!

SWARMING NEAR YOU

Locusts aren't limited to their home regions. They live — and eat! — all over the world. A giant swarm of these insects once descended on the North American prairie, consuming everything in its path. The Biggest Insect Swarm ever recorded occurred in Nebraska between July 20 – 30, 1874. This swarm of Rocky Mountain locusts covered 198,600 square miles and contained a jaw-dropping 12.5 *trillion* insects. Time to call in a bug's natural predator: the birds!

FACT:

The weight of this giant locust swarm would have been a whopping 50 billion pounds!

Feathered Friends

Look, up in the sky! No, it's not Superman — but you will see some super birds soaring among the clouds. Along our flight path, we'll spread our wings with the birds of prey and cool off with the fastest-swimming bird. Get set for takeoff — we've got a lot of bird-watching to do.

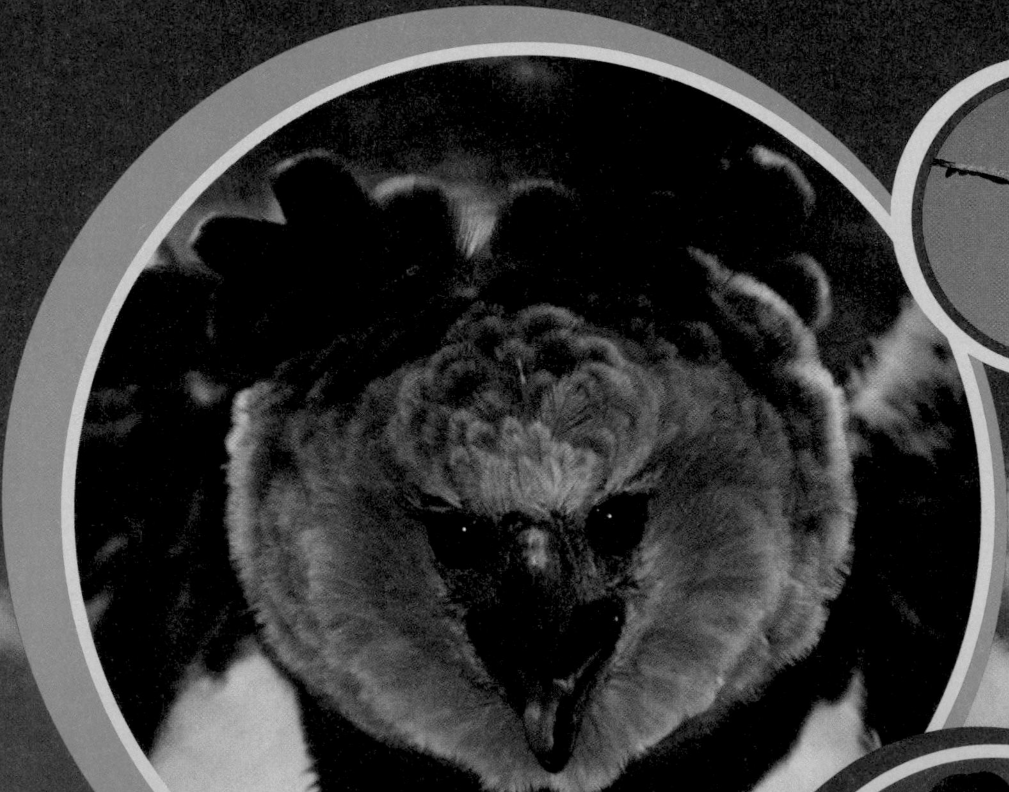

28

RECORD 16
Highest-Flying Bird

How high is too high for a bird to fly? There is a dangerous limit. The **Highest-Flying Bird** soared to its tragic altitude on November 29, 1973. A Ruppell's vulture collided with an airplane flying 37,000 feet — or more than 7 miles above the ground — over the African county of Abidjan, Ivory Coast. One of the plane's engines was damaged, but the aircraft landed safely. Although no humans were hurt, the bird died in the collision.

PREY PICK-UPS

Although a bird of prey, vultures do not kill animals. Instead, they hunt for the leftovers. This scavenger is nature's recycler. The vulture flies far from its nest and high above ground, searching for dead animals, known as carrion. Upon spotting a pick-up meal, a vulture circles the area to signal other vultures. A flock of vultures can devour an antelope's carcass within 20 minutes. Some species can even digest bones.

UP CLOSE

Birds of prey are hunters with wings.

Condors won't win the beauty pageant or the strength competition for birds of prey. Friendship doesn't interest a bird that communicates by noisy hissing, growling, and grunting at its nest mates. Yet these curiosity-seekers excel in graceful flight and exploration. Instead of flapping its gigantic wings (which measure more than 9 feet from tip to tip), the condor spreads them out and soars along on the breeze.

Raptor is another term for birds of prey.

RECORD 17
Rarest Bird of Prey

At one time, the skies over the western part of the United States were filled with a magnificent bird of prey called the California condor. By 1985, it was the **Rarest Bird of Prey**, with only 9 of them living in the wild.

A female California condor breeds only once every two years, and lays one egg at a time. Adult birds got into further trouble by flying into power poles. Early deaths and few babies added up to near-extinction.

Scientists began capturing and breeding the birds in captivity. After the chicks hatched, they were released back into the wild. A recent study shows the California condor is making a comeback: 49 exist in the wild with 99 captive birds waiting in the wings.

Tree-dwelling treats for harpies: monkeys, sloths, opossums, reptiles, and other birds.

HUNTING WITH HARPIES

Check your talons and let's go hunting with a harpy eagle.

🪶 Sharp eyesight spots our prey.

🪶 Short wings enable us to pursue quickly and flexibly among the tree branches.

🪶 Surprise attacks culminate in a swoop speed of 20 miles per hour.

🪶 This dive generates 13,500 foot-pounds of energy — more than twice the muzzle energy of a bullet fired from a rifle.

🪶 Grasping claws snare our prey and then it's up, up, and away!

RECORD 18
Strongest Bird of Prey

The female harpy eagle can kill and carry away an animal of equal or superior size, earning the record of **Strongest Bird of Prey**. These raptors measure 2 feet 8 inches long, and have a wingspan of 6 feet 6 inches. Females weigh between 14 and 20 pounds, while males weigh between 10 and 16 pounds. These hunters have the heaviest and stoutest legs. The female's lower legs can be as large in diameter as a child's wrist. The curved rear talons are about 5 inches long — the same size as a grizzly bear's claws! Harpy eagles nest in the rain forests of Central and South America, and the forests of southeastern Mexico, northern Argentina, and southern Brazil.

Penguins use their wings to fly through the sea, not through the sky.

There are 18 different species of penguin. The emperor penguin from Antarctica is the largest, growing up to 48 inches tall. The smallest penguin is the little blue penguin from New Zealand and Australia, struggling to reach 16 inches high. The familiar black-and-white bird keeps several records warm inside its mysterious tuxedo suit, including **Lowest Temperature Endured by a Bird.** The breeding emperor penguin survived -4° F and 16–47 mph wind speeds on the Antarctic sea ice.

Fastest Bird Swimmer

A penguin's body is perfectly shaped for swimming, and its flippers push and steer the bird while it hunts for its favorite food: fish! The speedy gentoo penguin outswims the other birds. The top speed of the **Fastest Bird Swimmer** is 17 miles per hour as it zips through Antarctica's chilly waters.

UP CLOSE

A penguin waddles upright because its short legs are placed far back on its body.

THE SECRET OF THE SUIT

In 1967, Dr. Bernard Stonehouse of the United Kingdom published a book based on his research that revealed penguins have the Highest Density of Feathers. Several types have 70 feathers per square inch. Each feather is controlled by its own set of small muscles. This intricate system keeps the penguin warm in cold or wet weather. On land, its feathers stand up straight to trap air. In water, the feathers lay flat to form a watertight barrier.

33

Birds of prey can be large and high-flying or tiny and super-shy.

Elf owls roam deserts and canyons in southeastern California, southern Arizona, southwestern New Mexico, and parts of Texas. Wintertime is spent in Mexico. These birds lay eggs inside abandoned woodpecker nests hollowed within oak trees and saguaro cacti. Daylight means hiding in its rented nest. Nighttime is the right time to hunt.

RECORD 20
Smallest Owl

The **Smallest Owl** measures an average of 4.75 to 5.5 inches long, weighs less than 1.75 ounces, and has a wingspan of only 9 inches. That's just about the size of a sparrow!

An elf owl is a successful hunter and gets all the water it needs from its diet. Mice, lizards, and insects are snatched from the air or scooped up from the ground.

If caught, elf owls play dead until freed.

We've saved the best for last! This chapter rounds up some of the most astonishing animals in the archives of Guinness World Records. Whip out the measuring tape (and scales) for the super-sized blue whale and the tiny hummingbird. Make sure your shoelaces are tied before running away from the dangerous bombardier beetle and king cobra. We haven't forgotten our favorite record-breaker in the pet category, either. Open this book WIDE for Lurch, a pet steer with horns as amazing as his life story. So here they are — five superstars of the wild kingdom!

A pet is a special friend who just happens to be an animal.

In Lurch's incredible life story, this pet is also a record-holder for an astonishing pair of horns! An African Watusi steer, Lurch was born in Missouri on October 11, 1995. He came to live with Janice Wolf at her Rocky Ridge Refuge in Gassville, Arkansas. At that time, he was just a cute and friendly 5-week-old steer. But by the time he turned 2 years old, something strange was going on above Lurch's ears.

RECORD 21
Largest Horn Circumference for a Steer

Lurch, through his human friend Janice Wolf, received his Guinness World Records certificate officially declaring him the record-holder of **Largest Horn Circumference for a Steer**. On May 6, 2003, his horns measured 37.5 inches around. Since then, Lurch broke his own record with his still-growing horns, now at 38 inches in circumference. His horns measure 7 feet from tip to tip, but not enough to claim the matching record for longest horns . . . yet.

Lurch's diet consists of hay, water, and lots of love!

> Lurch's best animal friend is a horse named Chance.

STAY AT HOME

Janice's home for Lurch and his animal friends is a special place named the Rocky Ridge Refuge. Janice takes her smaller pets — dogs, goats, and lambs — to meet people of all ages at schools or nursing homes. This type of visit is called "pet therapy," and both human and animal enjoy their shared time together. Lurch and his incredible horns won't fit through any doors, so he's more of a homebody waiting for people to stop by and visit him. He's worked with Janice to pose for pictures and give rides to his fans.

Elephants and tigers and polar bears are big, yet this one is a whale of a record-holder!

These records fit beneath its fins: Largest Animal Heart, Slowest Heartbeat in a Mammal, and Loudest Animal Sound.

Its heartbeat can be heard up to 20 miles away underwater. An adult human's heart beats about 70 times a minute. This gigantic heart beats between 4 and 8 times a minute! Its call is louder than a jet engine at 188 decibels. Scientists heard one call from 530 miles away. This mysterious creature is the ocean-dwelling blue whale.

RECORD 22
Largest Mammal

A blue whale can grow to a length of 115 feet, and weigh up to 352,000 pounds — that's as much as 27 adult elephants! Females are larger than males. One specimen measured 90 feet 6 inches long, and weighed 420,000 pounds. It was caught in the Southern Ocean, Antarctica, on March 20, 1947. The **Largest Mammal** must live in the ocean because the water supports its tremendous weight. On land, its own weight would crush its lungs.

BABY OVERBOARD!

Blue whales eat a tiny creature called krill. Whales suck water and krill into their mouths and then "catch" the krill with long bristles named baleen. One blue whale can eat 40 million krill a day!

If the adults are big, then the babies are not much smaller. A newborn blue whale is the Largest Offspring at 20 to 26 feet long, weighing more than 3 tons. Baby blue whales also grow faster. Every day, they add an inch and a half and gain about 200 pounds!

UP CLOSE

Stand inside the blue whale's rib cage: a heart the size of a small car powers this giant creature.

There's a saying that "good things come in small packages."

These records line the miniature nest of this species: Smallest Nest, Egg, and Bird plus Fastest Wing Beat.

The hummingbird comes in a variety of types and colors, but in one size only — tiny! Scientists don't think it's possible for any bird to weigh less than the bee hummingbird and survive. The bee hummingbird, specifically the male, is the Smallest Bird with an incredible weight of just 0.05 ounces — less than a penny! Its length measures only 2.25 inches, and half of that number is the bird's beak and tail.

RECORD 23
Smallest Nest and Egg

The vervain hummingbird builds a cozy little home, about half the size of a walnut shell, also known as the **Smallest Nest.** The bee hummingbird builds a deeper yet narrower nest about the size of a thimble. Naturally, the **Smallest Egg** is laid in these nests. Examples found were from the vervain hummingbird living in Jamaica. These two tiny eggs measured less than 0.39 inches in length and weighed a featherlight 0.0128 and 0.0132 ounces. Even the eggs of the "bigger" hummingbird types are only the size of a person's pinky fingernail!

Hummingbird Egg

Ostrich Egg

UP CLOSE

Hummingbirds hover by beating their wings fast — about 90 beats per second.

SUGAR-POWERED FLIGHT

Eating sugar gives humans a fast burst of energy, for a short time. Hummingbirds are all about energy in fast, short bursts. These birds eat insects and pollen for protein, but their main dietary staple is nectar, a sweet liquid from flowers. Nectar is full of sugar. Hummingbirds need this energy to keep their tiny bodies warm because this species generally has the fewest feathers on a bird. One hummingbird must eat every 10 minutes and consume more than half of its body weight.

FACT:

A big energy drain is flying. Extra-strong chest muscles, extra-light bones, and extra-flexible wings able to rotate at amazing speeds add up to make the hummingbird an aerobatic dynamo. The ruby-throated hummingbird can produce a wing beat rate of 200 beats per second, flying away with the record for Fastest Wing Beat of a bird.

A scaly monarch rules its kingdom with a fierce look and a deadly bite.

King cobras live in the tropical rain forests and grasslands of India, southern China, and Southeast Asia. They slither on land, up trees, and across water. If threatened, the king cobra hisses loudly, almost the sound of a dog's growl. It adopts a threat pose by standing up on its lower section and flattening its neck ribs into a hood. Other snakes' scales form patterns of false eyespots on their hoods to scare predators. The king cobra frightens its subjects without such tricks.

RECORD 24
Longest Venomous Snake

Every animal takes heed if the king cobra stands up. The **Longest Venomous Snake** measures 12 to 15 feet in length — making the king cobra long enough to look an adult human in the eye before it strikes! The snake has been known to pursue its prey in this position for up to a half mile. One bite contains only 0.2 fluid ounces of its powerful venom, yet it's enough to kill an elephant, or 20 people.

King cobras viciously protect their nests until their eggs hatch.

BIG GULP

This snake is a large-sized carnivore with a big appetite, and the mouth to match. Fortunately, humans aren't on its menu. The king cobra's favorite foods are other snakes (see the front cover for a mealtime snapshot). King cobras scent prey using their tongues. A snake's fangs deliver its venom, but this type of snake usually doesn't chew its food. The prey is swallowed whole — headfirst. The king cobra, like other snakes, can dislocate its jaw to devour a larger-sized creature. Strong acids in the snake's stomach take care of the digestion. One super-sized meal will satisfy the king cobra for months.

The King cobra's Latin name, *Ophiophagus hannah*, means "snake eater."

Animals have different ways of defending themselves.

They bite, scratch, make themselves look bigger, and even spit. A creature may be small, but its size does not indicate the power of its defense. The bombardier beetle cannot escape from danger as easily as other insects. A hard exoskeleton protects its outer body, but also slows down its flight response. While it spreads its wings, the bombardier beetle blasts its enemies with hot bug gas!

RECORD 25

Strangest Insect Defense Mechanism

The **Strangest Insect Defense Mechanism** is activated when a predator foolishly bugs this bug. The bombardier beetle's abdomen contains two chambers filled with different chemicals. These chemicals pour into a chamber and mix together before being sprayed out through the beetle's rotating rear nozzle. This defensive spray can be as hot as boiling water (212° F). The bombardier beetle can aim its spraying nozzle in any direction and hit its target with bull's-eye accuracy. The spray is accompanied by a loud popping sound audible to the human ear. A chemical reaction (hydrogen peroxide mixing with water and oxygen) causes the noise. The beetle can turn the scalding-hot spray on and off, 500 times every second!

Hot bug gas sprays from the beetle's rotating rear nozzle.

ZOOM OUT!

Although our book ends here, your exploration of these astonishing animals and their record-setting stories can continue among the online archives (www.guinnessworldrecords.com) and within the pages of *Guinness World Records.*

Go up close and get involved — it's your world!

Photo Credits

The publisher would like to thank the following for their
kind permission to use their photographs in this book:

Cover, title page (main) King Cobra © Belinda Wright/DRK PHOTO, (inset) Gaboon Viper © Joe McDonald/CORBIS; 3, 35 Whale Eye © Doug Allan/OSF; 4 Grouse © Tom Vezo/Peter Arnold, Inc.; 5 Giant Clam © Kiefner/PictureQuest, (top) Sea Horse © Georgette Douwma/Image State/PictureQuest, (bottom) Starfish © M. Timothy O'Keefe/Bruce Coleman, Inc./Alamy; 6 Starfish © Stephen Frink Collection/Alamy; 7 Starfish © Brandon Cole Marine Photography/Alamy; 8 Giant Clam © K. Byrne/Alamy; 9 Sea Horse © Stephen Frink Collection/Alamy; 10 Blue-Ringed Octopus © Gary Bell/SeaPics.com; 11 Copepod (top) © Roland Birke/Peter Arnold, Inc., (bottom) © Sinclair Stammers/Photo Researchers, Inc.; 12 (left) Gorilla © Gallo Images/CORBIS, (middle) Polar Bear © Daniel J. Cox/CORBIS, (right) Tiger © Tom Mangelsen/Minden Pictures; 13 Elephant © Daryl Balfour/Photo Researchers, Inc.; 14 Siberian Tiger © Andy Rouse/The Image Bank/Getty Images; 15 Tiger © Tim Davis/Stone/Getty Images, Bengal Cubs © Natacha Pisarenko/AP Wide World Photos; 16 Polar Bear and Cubs © Kennan Ward/CORBIS; 17 Polar Bear Standing © Steven Kazlowski/Peter Arnold, Inc.; 18 Gorillas in Nest © Rodrique Ngowi/AP Wide World Photos; 19 (top) Silverback Gorilla © Robert Pickett/Papilio/Alamy, (bottom) Koko © Ron Cohn/Newscom; 20 Beaver © Alan & Sandy Carey/Photo Researchers, Inc., Beaver Dam © David Hosking/Photo Researchers, Inc.; 21 (left) Spiny-Tailed Iguana © Steve Kaufman/Peter Arnold, Inc., (middle) Anaconda © Roland Seitre/Peter Arnold, Inc., (right) Cicada © G. I. Bernard/Photo Researchers, Inc.; 22 Boa Constrictor © Heinz Plenge/Peter Arnold, Inc./Alamy; 23 (top) Python © Renee Lynn/Photo Researchers, Inc., (bottom) Rattlesnake © Tom McHugh/Photo Researchers, Inc., (right) Mouse © Photodisc via SODA; 24 Spiny-tailed Iguana © C. Allan Morgan/Peter Arnold, Inc.; 25 (top) Lord Howe's Island Phasmids © Pavel German/Wildlife Images, (bottom) © Pavel German/Wildlife Images; 26 (top) Cicada © G. Mermet/Peter Arnold, Inc., (bottom) © Gary Meszaros/Photo Researchers, Inc.; 27 Locust (top) © A. Shay/OSF/Animals Animals, (inset) © Stephen Dalton/Photo Researchers, Inc., Swarm © Pierre Holtz/Reuters/Landov; 28 (left) Harpy Eagle © Kevin Schafer/CORBIS, (top) Vulture © Ross Warner/Alamy, (bottom) Penguin © Onne van der Wal/CORBIS; 29 Ruppell's Vulture © BIOS/Peter Arnold, Inc.; 30 California Condor © Tom McHugh/Photo Researchers, Inc.; 31 Harpy Eagle © Tui De Roy/Minden Pictures; 32 Penguins Jumping and Diving © Paul A. Souders/CORBIS; 33 Emperor Penguin © Kjell B. Sandved/Photo Researchers, Inc.; 34 (bottom) Elf Owl © Craig K. Lorenz/Photo Researchers, Inc., (right) © Kennan Ward/CORBIS; 35 Broad-Billed Hummingbird © Gerald C. Kelley/Photo Researchers, Inc.; 35, 36 Lurch © 2005 Drew Gardner/Guinness World Records; 37 Kids Riding Lurch courtesy of Janice Wolf; 38 Blue Whale Replica © David B. Fleetham/SeaPics.com; 39 Blue Whale with Young © Phillip Colla/SeaPics.com, (bottom) Blue Whale Rib Cage © Doug Perrine/SeaPics.com; 40 Ostrich and Hummingbird Eggs © Frans Lanting/Minden Pictures, Hummingbird Nest © Ron Austing, Frank Lane Picture Agency/CORBIS; 41 Ruby-Throated Hummingbird © Russell C. Hansen/Peter Arnold, Inc.; 42 King Cobra in Nest © Joe McDonald/Visuals Unlimited; 43 King Cobra Threat Pose © Peter B. Kaplan Photo Researchers, Inc.; 44 Bombardier Beetle © Handout/Reuters/Corbis; 45 Whale Tail © Gabriel Rojo/Nature Picture Library

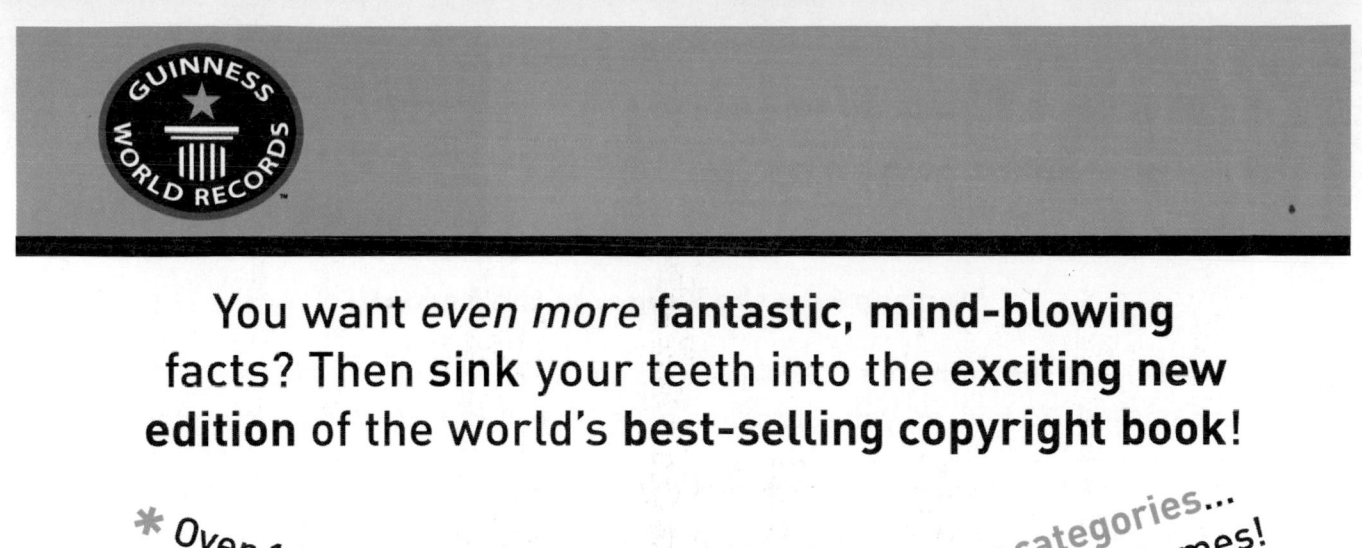

Be a Record-Breaker!

Message from the Keeper of the Records:

Record-breakers are the ultimate in one way or another — the youngest, the oldest, the tallest, the smallest. So how do you get to be a record-breaker? Follow these important steps:

1. Before you attempt your record, check with us to make sure your record is suitable and safe. Get your parents' permission. Next, contact one of our officials by using the record application form at www.guinnessworldrecords.com.

2. Tell us about your idea. Give us as much information as you can, including what the record is, when you want to attempt it, where you'll be doing it, and other relevant information.

   a) We will tell you if a record already exists, what safety guidelines you must follow during your attempt to break that record, and what evidence we need as proof that you completed your attempt.

   b) If your idea is a brand-new record nobody has set yet, we need to make sure it meets our requirements. If it does, then we'll write official rules and safety guidelines specific to that record idea and make sure all attempts are made in the same way.

3. Whether it is a new or existing record, we will send you the guidelines for your selected record. Once you receive these, you can make your attempt at any time. You do not need a Guinness World Record official at your attempt. But you do need to gather evidence. Find out more about the kind of evidence we need to see by visiting our website.

4. Think you've already set or broken a record? Put all of your evidence as specified by the guidelines in an envelope and mail it to us at: Guinness World Records, 338 Euston Road, London NWI 38D UK.

5. Our officials will investigate your claim fully — a process that can take up to a few weeks, depending on the number of claims we've received, and how complex your record is.

6. If you're successful, you will receive an official certificate that says you are now a Guinness World Record-holder!

Need more info? Check out the Kids' Zone on www.guinnessworldrecords.com for lots more hints and tips and some top record ideas that you can try at home or at school. Good luck!